THE INSTITUTE
Leader's Guide to ISO 55000

Authored by

Darrin J. Wikoff

Copyright © 2015 Eruditio, LLC

Institute at Patriots Point • 40 Patriots Point Road
Mt. Pleasant, SC 29464
Phone 843.375.8222 • www.theinstituteatpatriotspoint.com

ISBN-13: 978-1515399919

ISBN-10: 1515399915

LEADER'S GUIDE TO ISO 55001

Table of Contents

Strategic Asset Management Planning	5
Facilitating the Strategic Asset Management Plan	12
Alternative Approaches to Strategic Asset Management Planning	19
Management System Overview	25
Demonstrating Compliance to Management System Requirements	30
Organizational Context	31
Understanding the Needs and Expectations of Stakeholders	32
Determining the Scope of the Asset Management System	33
Leadership and Commitment	35
Organizational Roles, Responsibilities and Authorities	37
Actions to Address Risks and Opportunities for the Asset Management System	38
Asset Management Objectives	39
Planning to Achieve Asset Management Objectives	40
Resources	42
Competence	43
Awareness	44
Communication	45
Information Requirements	46
Documented Information: General Requirements	47
Documented Information: Creating and Updating	47
Documented Information: Control	48
Operational Planning and Control	48
Management of Change: Asset Related Changes	48
Management of Change: Asset Management Plan Changes	49
Outsourcing	49
Monitoring, Measurement, Analysis and Evaluation	50
Management Review	50
Nonconformity and Corrective Action	51
Preventive Action	52
Continual Improvement	53

Preface

This *Leader's Guide to ISO 55001* is the first of a series of books on *Leadership for Asset Management Excellence*. In collaboration with industry and academic leaders, this book is intended to be used as a resource for designing, administering and evaluating strategic asset management plans. This book is not accredited by the International Standards Organization, American National Standards Institute or any other governing standards body associated with ISO 55001. The views and perspectives expressed within this resource are those of the authors based on their collective experience as members of asset management councils and associations, and as business and community leaders in asset management.

About the Authors

Darrin J. Wikoff specializes in Organizational Change Management, Lean Manufacturing, Business Process Re-Engineering and Reliability Engineering. Since 2001, Darrin has continued to train, coach and mentor industrial leaders like Kraft Foods, Merck Pharmaceuticals, Mosaic Company, Alcoa World Wide Aluminum, Nissan and Schlumberger through the rigorous process of implementing and managing improvement initiatives in support of Lean Manufacturing. His ability to translate Lean and reliability engineering principles into real-world application has enabled these organizations to improve safety and environmental performance, increase production capacity and reduce operating costs. Darrin is widely known as a thought leader and has authored two other books, *"Centered On Excellence"* published by MRO-Zone in 2012 and the 7th edition of the *"Maintenance Engineering Handbook"* published by McGraw-Hill in 2008. He also served as a member of the U.S. Technical Advisory Group to ISO/TC 251 during the development of *ISO 55001: Asset Management – Management System – Requirements*.

Shon Isenhour is an engineering graduate of North Carolina State University, the past National Chairman of the Society of Maintenance and

Reliability Professionals (SMRP) and the current Chairman for the South Carolina chapter of the American Society for Training and Development (ATD, formerly ASTD). Since 2002, he has led improvement initiatives that have enabled his clients to succeed over their competitors in a changing global economy. As a Certified Maintenance & Reliability Professional (CMRP), Shon demonstrates superior technical subject matter knowledge and his ability as an experienced change management practitioner within such industries as primary metals, mining, pharmaceuticals, petrochemical, chemical processing and paper.

Brandon Weil has over 17 years of maintenance, reliability, leadership, and organizational change management experience as both a practitioner and consultant. He started his asset management career as an enlisted member of the U.S. Naval Nuclear Power Program and today is the Operations Manager and Lead Coach at Eruditio, LLC. During his time as a consultant and trainer, Brandon has participated in a multitude of large scale reliability improvement projects around the world, including a global implementation of "Reliability Excellence" across 31 Alcoa Primary Metals locations from 2003-2007. Brandon holds a B.S in Business and is a Certified Maintenance and Reliability Professional (CMRP). His passion for learning is obvious to his students, and he has been recognized by multiple Fortune 500 companies for his unique ability to translate difficult technical concepts into practical, sustaining skills.

Strategic Asset Management Planning

"Using an integrated management systems approach allows an organization's asset management system to be built on elements of its other management systems, such as for quality, environment, health and safety, and risk management. Building on existing systems can reduce the effort and expense involved in creating and maintaining an asset management system. It can also improve integration across different disciplines and improve cross-functional coordination."

~ *ISO 55000: Section 2.6 Integrated Management System Approach*

A **Strategic Asset Management Plan (SAMP)** is nothing more than evidence of the "Documented Information" requirements and specifies how asset management objectives align, support, or will convert to strategic organizational objectives. In doing so, the SAMP also outlines the "Key Activities" required to achieve said objectives, of which all asset management plans will subsequently include. Each key activity is further defined within the plan relative to the resources required, cost considerations and timeline for implementation and realization of objectives.

The Strategic Asset Management Plan should originate from the organization's business plan, demand plan, asset utilization plan or any other document that defines, in detail, the business drivers and the impact they have on the financial and image growth of the business. Business drivers, and the focus given, should be balanced in order to grow the business uniformly in all directions to prevent the encroachment of unwanted external risks (e.g. "competitive pressures").

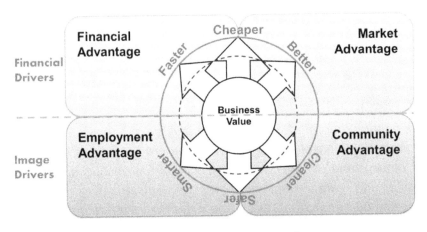

Figure 1- Competitive "Value"
(Source: Centered On Excellence by Darrin J Wikoff)

The challenges we face in everyday business are the result of external competitive pressures, as well as, internal constraints, or said simply, the result of one company doing something better than the competition. Your SAMP should be a holistic approach to maximizing your business' potential to be the best. The design of your asset management system should be based on identifying fundamental, value-adding business processes, quantifying gaps that prevent achievement of strategic business goals, followed by tactical improvements to optimize asset and asset management performance.

Leadership for asset management has a fundamental decision to make. You can chose to achieve the benchmarks set by others, or you can chose to sustain a level of performance that is better than that of your competition. The latter requires a mindset that is never satisfied with the status quo and is constantly looking for opportunities to improve and apply pressure outward to the competition. The mindset of the

"Excellent" organization is one of continuous evaluation and refinement of asset and asset management performance goals.

The "competitive value" of a business is nothing more than a systematic approach to identifying the overlying objectives that will enable the business to comprehensively expand its growth potential beyond the achievements of its competitors.

The focus of this model is to organize asset management objectives based on four categories, Finance, Customers, Community and Employees, relative to your stakeholder requirements. Objectives should be balanced in order to drive performance improvement in two equal directions, the financial health of the business and overall image of the business.

Financial growth is based on the organization's ability to reduce the cost of operating through focused improvements in overhead, maintenance and material costs. Financial growth is also reliant on the business's ability to improve capacity through higher levels of availability, production rate and quality. These capacity improvements must be equally focused on product and service development based on customer demand.

Image growth, on the other hand, is based on the organization's ability to develop intellectual capital within its own business through training, strength-based organizational structures and performance management, and the business' ability to expand its license to operate within the community based on environmental, health and safety performance and a reputation for quality employment.

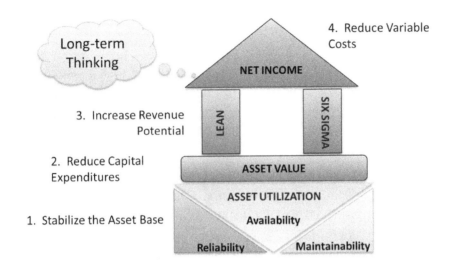

Figure 2 - Alignment of Asset Management Objectives

An equally important consideration when crafting your SAMP is the order and priority of asset management objectives, and their subsequent asset management plans. Take Figure 2 as the mental model for SAMP. The proverbial "Lean House" stands as a representation of the financially driven strategic objectives of the organization. At the top of the house is the ultimate value proposition for the business, Profitability (i.e. Net Income) – Revenue minus Cost. We can conclude that our asset management objectives would be to reduce the variable costs associated with producing the value stream, while at the same time optimizing the potential capacity within the value stream to generate revenue.

But what about the foundation upon which the house is built? That's the "asset base" and it is a very important part of the financial equation. If your organization is using a metric such as Return On Assets (ROA), every dollar of profit is divided by the asset base – Average Asset Value. Return On Assets is calculated as:

$$ROA = \frac{Net\ Income}{Average\ Asset\ Value}$$

This type of metric is in fact evaluating your asset management system performance. "How well does Company A generate a profit from its asset base compared to Company B?", and "Are Company A's management systems as effective as Company B's?" are the questions we answer with this metric.

Relative to physical assets specifically, the asset base is only as strong as it is Available to be operated – to generate revenue producing services or products within the value stream. Availability is the result of the asset base being both Reliable – the probability of conforming to the desired function without failure – and Maintainable – the ability of your management system to restore functionality after a non-conformance has occurred. Our asset management objectives within the SAMP should include a flavor of Reliability, Availability and Maintainability in the sense that it is important to the business to create a stabile foundation upon which to produce a profit.

Secondarily, our asset management objectives should also focus on reducing the asset base, making it smaller and thus reducing the divisibility of profits. Eliminating redundant, underutilized and unnecessary assets from the asset base or reducing the volume of replacement assets, such as spare parts, from the asset base will increase your organization's financial "competitive value", assuming profits do not decline within the same fiscal period.

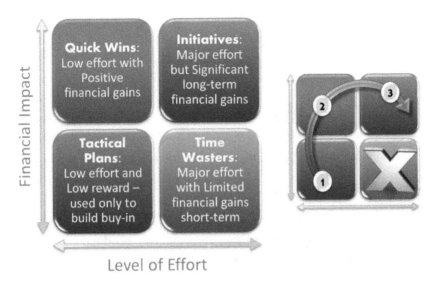

Figure 3 - Prioritizing Asset Management Objectives

Our first step when developing the SAMP is to document the value propositions for our business and align our asset management focus to achieve these organizational objectives. Once the organizational context is defined, and our asset management objectives are known, we need to provide a priority for each objective that will determine the order in which "Key Activities", "Key Resources" and other considerations are allocated. These priorities should also govern the order in which asset management plans at the tactical level are designed and implemented. In essence, providing a priority to your asset management objectives is the first step in building the design and implementation timeline.

Prioritization of asset management objectives should follow a "1-2-3-Let it Be" mantra. Priority 1 objectives are those that will help build buy-in, awareness and support for the asset management system long-term. These objectives are primarily associated with the organizational and individual change management plans, and should require a lower level of effort as a whole to design and implement. It should be understood that these objectives may not have a long-term impact on the strategic organizational objectives; however, these objectives should be expected to reduce the time it takes to see a positive impact on organizational objectives.

Priority 2 asset management objectives are those that will deliver an immediate, "quick win" impact to organizational objectives. Similar to Priority 1, these objectives should require lower levels of effort to design and implement, and should be limited to an isolated number of resources that reside under the direct responsibility and authority of the asset owner or manager.

Priority 3 asset management objectives are the more complex initiatives within the SAMP. These objectives require extensive asset management planning to coordinate resources, role responsibilities and key activities. The increased level of effort must be reconciled by long-term, significant financial or image gains to the business.

"1-2-3-Let it Be." If your asset management objective doesn't fall into one of the first three priorities, and a major level of effort is required for asset management planning with limited short-term financial gain to the business, then you may consider the objective to be a "Time Waster". Time wasters consume resources and restrict your organization's ability to tackle more meaningful opportunities. Time wasters require the same level of effort as the "Initiatives", but lack the benefits necessary to maintain Top Management support and buy-in. If the risk driving the objective is noteworthy enough to require asset management planning, steps should be taken to identify the "Quick Qin" objectives as milestones within the overall strategic plan.

Facilitating the Strategic Asset Management Plan

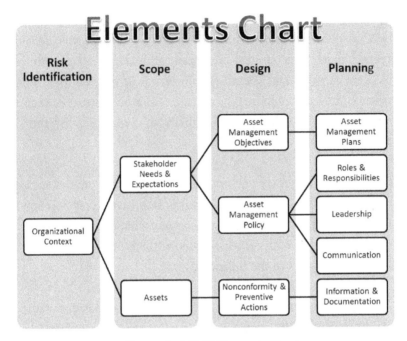

Figure 4 - SAMP Elements Chart

The Strategic Asset Management Plan (SAMP) will transition through four phases over the course of its life cycle, with each phase building a more definitive understanding of the risks inherent within and surrounding the organization, and the management system requirements to effectively mitigate the risks. Once the fourth and final phase of the SAMP is complete, preparation begins for implementation.

The four phases of strategic asset management planning are:

- Business Planning,
- Risk Identification,
- Scope Definition, and
- Design and Planning

Business Planning

In the first phase, Top Management participates in the development of a "Business Model Canvas" that visually illustrates the needs of the business, and its stakeholders, and begins to outline the business provisions for asset management.

The canvas begins at the center of the business, the "Value Proposition". Here, Top Management quantitatively defines the financial and image drivers of the business in terms of both internal and external stakeholder requirements. The value propositions answer the question, "what is our business?" As an Asset Management stakeholder, you might say your business is "to ensure value through risk mitigation" or "to manage the risk of non-conformance". However, Top Management would define the value propositions similar to:

- Provide a high-quality product at a low-cost to the consumer
- Provide meaningful employment in a safe environment
- Increase market share above 60% through on-time delivery
- Reduce product defects by 10% through improved reliability

The canvas unfolds to the right and documents the external stakeholders, often referred to as "Customer Segments", but may also include regulatory agencies or shareholders who will benefit from the value propositions and will ultimately determine the success of the business' ability to deliver the intended outcomes.

To the left of the value propositions, Top Management defines the internal and external stakeholders that influence the intended outcomes. The internal stakeholders are thought to be either "Key Partners" who must be engaged in decision making processes in order to accomplish the specified "Key Activities" associated with each value proposition, or "Key

Resources" who are responsible for implementing the associated activities.

At the bottom of the canvas, Top Management begins to document the business liabilities, in terms of "Cost Structures" necessary to implement the key activities, and the "Revenue Streams" that are at risk and will serve as the initial definition of risk consequences for further management planning.

Figure 5 provides a high-level example of the Business Model Canvas approach to business planning for asset management. When developing your business canvas it is important that each stakeholder group be present and represented in order to align the objectives and activities associated with your SAMP with stakeholder requirements.

Make business planning a visual exercise in order to maintain a collaborative and unified focus on the plan. Refrain from using computer software, spreadsheets and other media that restricts the participants' view of the entire plan. The outcome of the business planning phase of the SAMP is to walk away with a clear definition of what the business is, and how asset management supports the business in terms of value.

Figure 5 - The Business Model Canvas

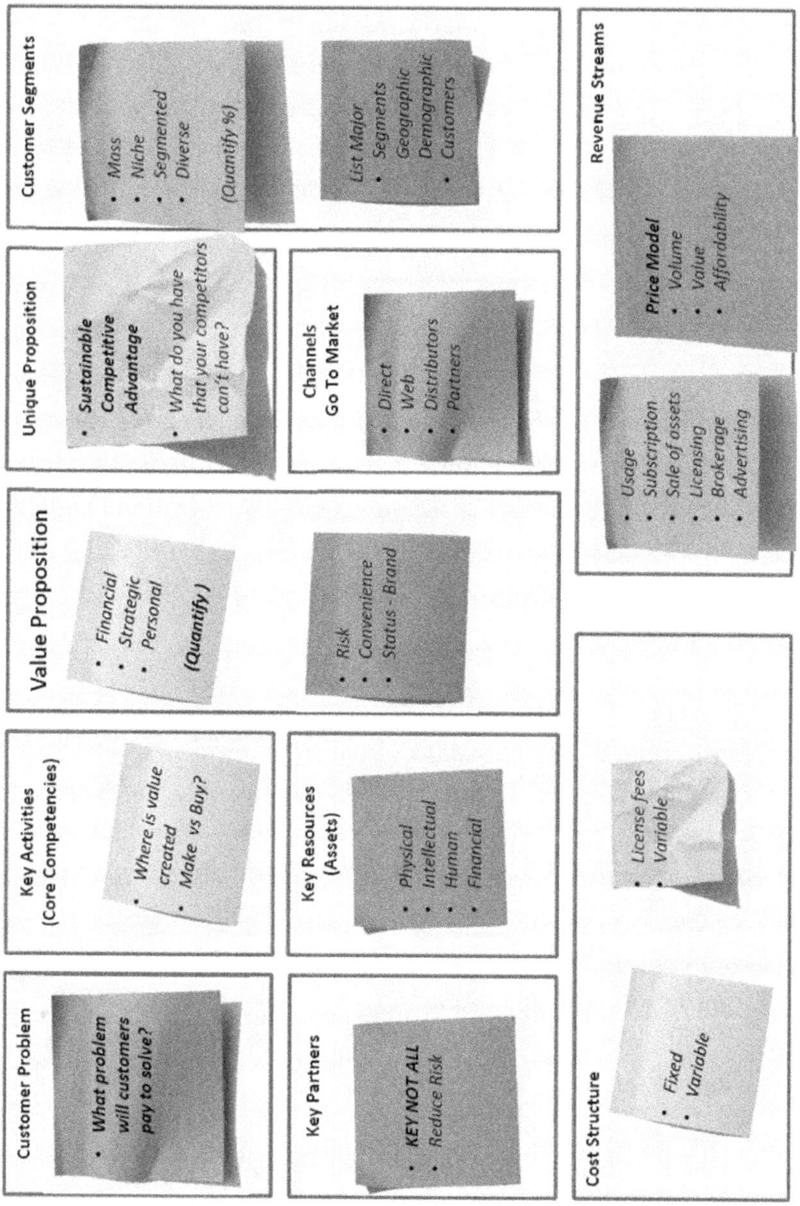

Customer Segments
- Mass
- Niche
- Segmented
- Diverse

(Quantify %)

List Major
- Segments
- Geographic
- Demographic
- Customers

Revenue Streams

Price Model
- Volume
- Value
- Affordability

- Usage
- Subscription
- Sale of assets
- Licensing
- Brokerage
- Advertising

Unique Proposition

Sustainable Competitive Advantage
- What do you have that your competitors can't have?

Channels Go To Market
- Direct
- Web
- Distributors
- Partners

Value Proposition
- Financial
- Strategic
- Personal

(Quantify)

- Risk
- Convenience
- Status - Brand

Key Activities (Core Competencies)
- Where is value created
- Make vs Buy?

Key Resources (Assets)
- Physical
- Intellectual
- Human
- Financial

License fees Variable

Customer Problem
- What problem will customers pay to solve?

Key Partners
- KEY NOT ALL
- Reduce Risk

Cost Structure
- Fixed
- Variable

Risk Identification

The next phase of strategic asset management planning is intended to define the risks associated with not delivering the intended outcomes. ISO 31000 defines risk as *"the effect of uncertainty on the ability of an organization to meet its objectives"*. In this context, our planning process must define both the "effect", in terms of consequences to the business, and the level of "uncertainty". Risk, as a formula, is:

$$Risk = \frac{Value}{Time}$$

Consequence or the "effect" is quantified by the revenue or value streams defined in the Business Model Canvas, or the lack thereof. Uncertainty deals with the likelihood or probability that the organization will deliver the intended outcomes, without adjustments to existing management systems, within the desired time period. Uncertainty as such is a measure of time.

This is a very interesting departure from the common understanding of risk. Most professionals only think of risk in terms of what happens when something goes wrong, instead of trying to quantify the impact of <u>not knowing what will go wrong</u>. Risk management, in turn, is *"the range of activities an organization intentionally undertakes to understand and reduce the effects of uncertainty"* [ISO 31000]. Relative to asset management planning, risk management is the process of analyzing asset performance or asset management system performance relative to the strategic objectives (i.e. "Value Propositions") of the business, thus removing the uncertainty.

A practical example of risk identification within the SAMP process is to evaluate the impact asset availability, as a measure of time and uncertainty, has on the specified revenue potential of the business. If the intended outcome of the revenue stream is 100 units based on an asset availability of 85%, but the current availability is only 68%, the risk of not knowing what will go wrong is a loss of 29 units. The equation for this type of risk identification would be:

$$Risk = \left(\frac{Target\ Revenue}{Target\ Availability}\right) - \left(\frac{Target\ Revenue}{Current\ Availability}\right)$$

$$Risk = \left(\frac{100}{0.85}\right) - \left(\frac{100}{0.68}\right)$$

$$Risk =- 29\ Units$$

The desired result of the risk identification phase is to develop a risk register that can be used to evaluate potential risks and make decisions impacting the performance of assets and the asset management system. Is a loss of 29 units significant to the business? Is this a risk that needs to be managed? If your revenue stream is based in a market that can sell every unit produced, and the cost of production is fixed, then yes this might be a risk worth managing. The risk register should define these decisions as a reflection of stakeholder requirements.

Scope Definition

So, what has the potential to go wrong? What assets have the ability to impact availability within the previous example? Answering these questions is the intent of the third phase of the SAMP process, Scope Definition.

Documenting the scope of the asset management system expands the original list of assets captured in the "Key Resources" portion of the Business Model Canvas to more precisely define those assets that have the most significant chance of causing an unintended consequence. In the least, the scope defines those assets that have the greatest level of performance uncertainty.

In this phase, with regards to physical assets specifically, validation of asset relationships occurs – known as the "Asset Catalog" or "Asset Hierarchy" – and a formal "Criticality Analysis" is conducted in order to differentiate one asset within the catalog from another in terms of consequence or probability of non-conformance – not doing what it is intended to do. Qualitatively, the criticality analysis ranks the in-scope assets in terms of the perceived impact on organizational objectives. Quantitatively, reliability and availability modeling can be used to further define the level of uncertainty within groupings of assets (e.g. Asset System, Asset Type, value streams or product groups).

Design and Planning

The fourth phase is where Top Management and stakeholder representatives determine how in-scope assets will be managed. We can break this final phase of strategic planning into two sub-processes, designing the asset management system, and planning for system implementation.

Design is focused on documenting the methods by which assets will be managed. Design is where the asset management objectives are defined based on the identified risks. For example, using the previous example, one objective might be "to ensure 85% asset availability within the Product X revenue stream".

Designing the asset management system also includes the governing principles established by Top Management as evidence of asset management policies, and clearly defined business processes that illustrate how each stakeholder or group of stakeholders is meant to interact and engage in the asset management system.

Planning is a deeper dive into the mechanics of the asset management system design. This is where detailed asset management plans, such as an

"Equipment Maintenance Plan", are documented as evidence of decisions to mitigate known risks.

Planning for implementation will also document the role responsibilities of each stakeholder relative to the day-to-day execution of asset management plans and their activities, as defined by business processes. Planning for implementation also requires Top Management and stakeholder representatives to document the required information used within the business processes and the governance structures necessary to report asset management system performance to stakeholders and make decisions that impact performance.

Alternative Approaches to Strategic Asset Management Planning

While ISO 55001 is an internationally adopted consensus standard that reflects the current wisdom and experience of asset management professionals and thought leaders around the globe, the manner in which compliance is achieved can and should be scalable based on the maturity and needs of your organization. Auditors are looking for documented evidence of each requirement, not the approach.

Starting with a Business Plan

In the event that your organization already has a formally documented business plan that clearly defines the measurable expectations of Top Management and stakeholders, a less formal SWOT Analysis could be facilitated in order to document the organizational context risks needing to be managed. This is a common practice for organizations that are less focused on physical assets and who have a greater opportunity to manage human, intellectual or intangible asset risks. The SWOT Analysis is also a good alternative in circumstances where asset management plans already exists and Top Management's responsibility for strategic planning is to evaluate where current risk controls are or could fail to meet stakeholder expectations.

Guide to S.W.O.T. Analysis

Strengths:	Weaknesses:
Consistently perform business practices that meet the desired Mission. Consistent performance levels that reflect Mission values.	Current business practices that prevent the Mission from being achieved. Business performance levels that are not consistent with Mission values.
Opportunities:	Threats:
Opportunities that will exist if the Global Company can overcome known weaknesses.	External or internal limitations or competitive pressures that may prevent improvement to meet desired Mission.

S.W.O.T. Analysis (Example)

Strengths:	Weaknesses:
• Plant capacity is sold out • Product mix is 1 specification to 1 product line (1:1) • Production efficiency is > 95% • Employee turnover is < 2% per	• Uptime is < 80% • Production Quality is < 85% • Maintenance costs are > 5% of RAV • No formal training program
Opportunities:	Threats:
• 1% OEE = 1,600 Tons Per Day, or $456,000 additional revenue per day • Maintenance Costs at 5% RAV = $23,000,000, a savings of $12,000,000 annually	• Business processes are not clearly defined • Specific product defects are not recorded or trended • Equipment work and failure history is limited • No formal PM/PdM Program • Current organizational structure does not support formalized training

Figure 6 - SWOT Analysis
(Source: Centered On Excellence by Darrin J Wikoff)

When using an alternative approach like the SWOT Analysis, be mindful to clearly link the identified business risks, and the stakeholders that provided the asset performance expectation, to your asset management objectives. The analysis itself is insufficient evidence. Where possible, break the current business plan into strategic organizational objectives and analyze each objective separately. Similar to the Business Model Canvas, there must be sufficient documentation of the "Key Activities" and associated resources, performance evaluation criteria and infrastructure requirements (e.g. Cost Structures). Below is an outline to follow when using this alternative SWOT Analysis approach:

1. Strategic Organizational Objective
    1.1. SWOT Analysis
        1.1.1. Asset Management Objective(s)
            1.1.1.1. Current Process or Plan Gap Analysis
                1.1.1.1.1. Performance Evaluation Criteria (i.e. KPI)
                1.1.1.1.2. Resource Requirements
                1.1.1.1.3. Information & Documentation Requirements
                1.1.1.1.4. Cost Structure

Planning for New Installation

In many cases, Top Management decides to use a new installation as a proving ground for ISO 55001 as an isolated "pilot" of asset management principles and requirements. In such instances, the risks have been identified through the Front End Loading (FEL) processes of the engineering department or firm, and stakeholder requirements are well documented in terms of User Requirements Specifications, Functional Specifications and Design Specifications. The asset management objectives and subsequent planning will be to validate that the build, installation, operation and performance of the new asset(s) will meet the documented specifications.

Validation, as defined by the Food and Drug Administration's (FDA) "Process Validation: General Principles and Practices" is the method of establishing documented evidence that provides a high degree of certainty that a specific process, system or asset will consistently produce a product meeting its pre-determined specifications and quality attributes.

The concept of validation was first developed for physical assets and derived from engineering management of change practices used in the delivery of large pieces of equipment that would be manufactured, tested, delivered and accepted according to both user and functional specifications. The use of validation spread to other areas of industry, including petro-chemical and food and beverage, after several large-scale problems highlighted the potential risks in the design of products.

As a best practice for managing asset performance relative to product quality, seasoned asset managers have adopted the asset validation methodology in an effort to proactively identify procedures for testing components prior to installation, verifying that operating practices are not inducing defects which could affect the product, and proving the effectiveness of maintenance plans. The asset validation procedure is also the first step towards establishing a management of change process (MOC), which is adequate evidence of ISO 55001 requirements governing the management of non-conformance.

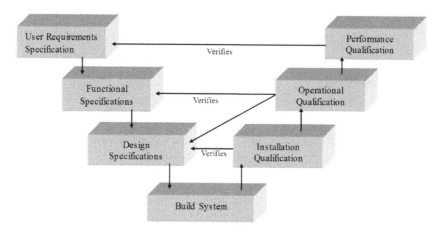

Figure 7 - Validation Key Activities

The validation scope, boundaries and responsibilities for each activity must be documented and approved in the validation plan, which should be based on identified asset and non-asset related risks to ensure that the scope of the validation is appropriate for the complexity and importance of the equipment or process. The validation plan must ensure that all aspects of the process and associated personnel and equipment are qualified relative to efficacy and quality. Qualification includes the following steps:

- Design Qualification (DQ) – Demonstrates that the proposed design (or the existing design for an off-the-shelf item) will satisfy all the requirements that are defined and detailed in the User Requirements Specification (URS). Satisfactory execution of the design qualification is a mandatory requirement before construction (or procurement) of the new design can be authorized.

- Installation Qualification (IQ) – Demonstrates that the process or equipment meets all specifications, is installed correctly, and all required components and documentation needed for continued operation are installed and in place.

- Operational Qualification (OQ) – Demonstrates that all facets of the process, equipment and manufacturing personnel are integrated and functioning correctly in accordance with the design and functional specifications.

- Performance Qualification (PQ) – Demonstrates that the process or assets perform as intended, in a consistent manner over time, in accordance with the user specifications.

- Maintenance Qualification (MQ) – A subset of the Performance Qualification, that demonstrates the organization's ability to detect asset-related risks which could potentially impact product quality, personnel safety or release hazardous materials to the environment.

The Validation Plan is a document that describes how and when the validation program will be executed in your facility. It is the asset management plan that outlines the governing principles involved in the qualification of a new asset installation, defines the areas and systems to be validated (i.e. Scope), and provides documentation for achieving and maintaining stakeholder requirements. At a minimum, to be compliant with ISO 55001 requirements, the plan should include the process and decision making framework for risk identification, acceptance testing criteria, resource requirements and qualification standards, and a means to inform stakeholders when the identified specifications are unable to be met.

Chapter 2

Management System Overview

"Asset management enables an organization to realize of value from assets in the achievement of its organizational objectives. What constitutes value will depend on these objectives, the nature and purpose of the organization and the needs and expectations of its stakeholders. Asset management supports the realization of value while balancing financial, environmental and social costs, risk, quality of service and performance related to assets."

~ *ISO 55000: Section 2.2 Benefits of Asset Management*

This chapter will focus on defining the terms associated with ISO 55001 and provide insight into how these terms interrelate within the Strategic Asset Management Plan (SAMP).

Assets exist within an organization to provide <u>value</u> to the organization and its stakeholders. Assets, by this definition are:

- Any item that has a potential value within an organization,
- Any item that has an actual value to an organization,
- A group of items that has a potential or actual value, regardless of the individual item value (e.g. Asset System),
- A group of items that have a common characteristic that translates into value, regardless of the individual item value (e.g. Asset Type).

Value is defined by the organization that has accountability for the asset during a specific period within the asset life cycle. Refer to Figure 9 to determine the period of asset accountability. Value can be:

- Tangible or intangible,
- Financial or non-financial,
- Equity or liability (gains or losses), and
- Risk or benefit.

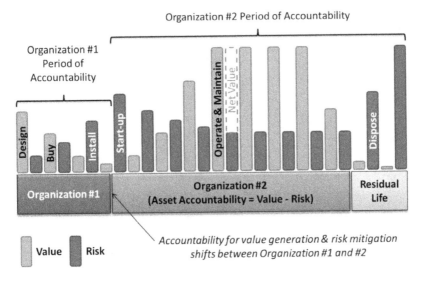

Figure 9 - Asset Life Cycle - Whole Life View

Both value and the period of asset accountability may change throughout the asset life cycle, which begins at asset creation and ends when the asset no longer has value to any single organization.

Asset Management provides <u>assurance</u> that assets will fulfill their required purpose relative to the stated value. Therefore, asset management can be defined as the coordinated activity of an organization to protect, optimize or realize value from assets during the period of accountability. Methods of assuring value include:

- Balancing cost,
- Controlling risk, and
- Monitoring performance of both assets and the asset management system.

Key Activities performed by an organization as demonstration of asset management can be defined as:

- Providing context (i.e. scope),
- Planning,
- Implementation,
- Support,
- Operation,
- Performance evaluation, and
- Improvement.

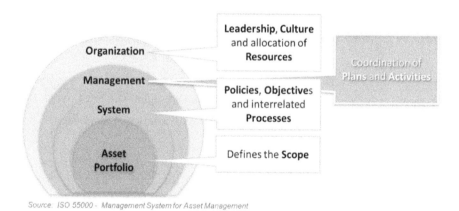

Source: ISO 55000 - Management System for Asset Management

Figure 8 - Asset Management Landscape

The **Asset Management System** translates organizational objectives, relative to value, into technical and financial decisions by way of:

- Policies,
- Plans,
- Processes,
- Organizational structures, and
- Resources.

The asset management system should be integrated with other management systems in place by an organization whenever possible.

Asset Management Policies formally express Top Management's intentions and direction within an organization as governing principles or guidelines by which the asset management system should be administered. Top Management refers to those individuals or roles that have the power to delegate authority and provide the necessary resources.

Asset Management Plans are documents that translate policy into actions or tasks, including resource requirements and timelines, for a specific asset in order to achieve the stated value and organizational objectives.

Leadership and Culture are determining factors when considering the organization's ability to administer the asset management system and achieve the organizational objectives, relative to value. Leadership activities include, but are not limited to:

- Defining roles, responsibilities and authorities,
- Allocating resources,
- Ensuring stakeholders are aware, competent and empowered, and
- Aligning the asset management system with stakeholder requirements.

The term "Stakeholder" refers to a person or organization that has the potential to be impacted by, or may perceive them as being impacted by, a decision or key activity associated with the management system.

The term "Resources" refers to personnel, information, information technology, documents and other supporting infrastructure deemed necessary within the documented asset management plans.

LEADER'S GUIDE TO ISO 55001

Chapter 3

Demonstrating Compliance to Management System Requirements

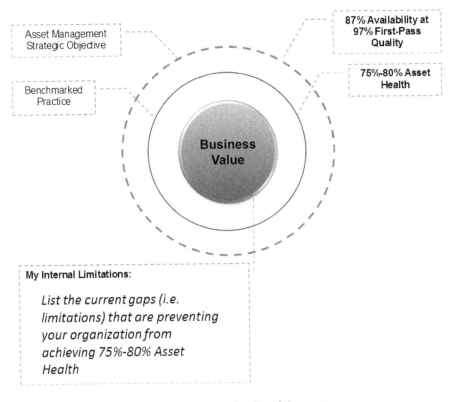

Figure 10 - Organizational Context
(Source: Centered On Excellence by Darrin J Wikoff)

In this chapter we will define each management system requirement, in the order they appear in the standard document, and describe the manner of compliance. For each requirement, we will list examples that may be presented to auditors as evidence of compliance, and provide a means for performance evaluation based on a scale from "Level 1 – Non-compliant" through "Level 3 – Compliant" to "Level 5 – Excellence".

Organizational Context

Demonstrate that your organization has considered internal and external risk factors that have the potential to influence business outcomes when determining the objectives of your asset management system. Internal risk refers to gaps in internal processes, and external risk refers to political, economic, regulatory or other factors beyond the local organization's control.

Evidence of Compliance:

- A documented process exists to determine both internal and external risk factors and their potential impact on organizational objectives. Such processes may include but are not limited to a PEST Analysis, SWOT Analysis, Business Model Canvas, Business Planning, Demand Planning or Enterprise Resource Planning.

Level 1	Level 2	Level 3	Level 4	Level 5
No formal analysis of Asset Management scope relative to organizational strategic objectives.	Financial impact of Asset Management scope understood by Top Management.	All internal limitations and external constraints that impact organizational strategic objectives identified.	Organizational and individual change risks identified. Change management plans exist to mitigate risks.	Asset Management strategy and plans are routinely evaluated to identify risks to organizational strategic objectives.

- The Strategic Asset Management Plan clearly links asset management objectives to organizational objectives and other management system objectives, such as ISO 9001 or the financial system.

Level 1	Level 2	Level 3	Level 4	Level 5
No business case has been developed.	A business case has been built using artificial cost savings targets.	Financial gains are defined by benchmarks. Top Management understands and supports improvement opportunity.	Asset Management Objectives are documented in other management system plans as enablers or co-contributors to organizational goals.	Stakeholders communicate short-term and long-term benefit of Asset Management relative to their business requirement.

Understanding the Needs and Expectations of Stakeholders

Demonstrate that your organization has identified both the stakeholder and their requirements when determining asset management objectives, and provide evidence that the stakeholder is integrated in decision making processes. Stakeholders may be external to the organization, including government agencies, shareholders and customers.

Evidence of Compliance:

- The Strategic Asset Management Plan includes a "Stakeholder Analysis" or similar document as a formal process for the management of internal and external stakeholders.

Level 1	Level 2	Level 3	Level 4	Level 5
Stakeholder is casually aware of the initiative.	Stakeholder provided input when developing the Asset Management objectives.	Stakeholder demonstrates an ability to influence the execution of Asset Management plans in order to drive the intended result.	Stakeholder routinely participates in decision making processes that impact Asset Management and organizational outcomes.	Stakeholder is committed to Asset Management as a sponsor and holds himself and others accountable for its outcomes

Determining the Scope of the Asset Management System

Demonstrate that the identification of "Assets" within the asset management system is consistent with the Asset Management Policy and other management systems, if applicable.

Evidence of Compliance:

- "Asset Catalogs" are clearly documented and reflect all management system policies governing physical and financial "Assets", including vendor managed inventories and repairable spares.

Level 1	Level 2	Level 3	Level 4	Level 5
No association of assets within the asset register.	Some informal grouping of assets exists within the asset register. Criteria for grouping is based on physical relationship to area, process, or geography.	Assets grouped by functional parent / child relationships and conforms to ISO 14224.	Level III plus asset catalog includes asset attributes, BOM, and functional specifications.	Level IV plus a formal MOC process exists to ensure accuracy and integrity of asset information and data reporting.

Document within the Strategic Asset Management Plan those assets that are governed by the asset management system and the rational for determining applicability and scope. Demonstrate the link between asset management decisions and other management systems, if applicable.

Evidence of Compliance:

- A documented process exists for determining "Asset Criticality" that includes requirements identified by all stakeholders. "Assets" are ranked relative to their impact on organizational objectives of stakeholder requirements.

Level 1	Level 2	Level 3	Level 4	Level 5
No formal criticality analysis has been performed; "criticality" is perception-based.	Criticality analysis performed by functional area or department with limited granularity.	Facility or plant wide criticality analysis performed to formally rank all assets. Granularity constrained by limitations of CMMS or EAMS.	Level III but good granularity exists to identify asset and Asset Management system risks and priorities for expenditures.	Level IV plus asset criticality is routinely reviewed against organizational strategic objectives.

Leadership and Commitment

Demonstrate by way of formal meeting agendas or communication schedules the means by which Top Management integrates the asset management system with other management systems within the organization.

> Evidence of Compliance:

- The Strategic Asset Management Plan includes a "Communication Plan" or similar document as a formal process for identifying stakeholder messaging, frequency of messaging and delivery method.

Level 1	Level 2	Level 3	Level 4	Level 5
No formal message from Top Management beyond the statement of an Asset Management initiative.	Top Management connects internally the linkage between Asset Management and business strategic objectives.	Level II plus Top Management actively participates in cross-functional meetings and processes that influence Asset Management objectives.	Level III plus Top Management connects Asset Management system expectations to relevant external stakeholders.	Level IV plus Top Management routinely evaluates understanding and ability of Asset Management objectives and targets.

(Includes Policy clause) Demonstrate through documented processes that Top Management is required to participate in setting policies and making decisions that impact asset management objectives.

Evidence of Compliance:

- A documented Asset Management Policy exists and is formally endorsed or authorized by Top Management. This policy should be governed and administered similar to other organizational policies. The policy includes core asset management principles, role descriptions, decision making frameworks, risk management frameworks and governance structures, including the date and frequency of a formal policy review.

Level 1	Level 2	Level 3	Level 4	Level 5
Alignment to Asset Management policies is voluntary; non-compliance is not addressed.	Old performance measures and incentives are in place that conflict with Asset Management policies. Auditing of Asset Management policies occurs ad hoc.	Performance measures and incentives are aligned with Asset Management policies, and non-compliance is formally documented.	Level III plus routine auditing of Asset Management policies.	Level IV plus Top Management provides the necessary resources for continued training and coaching of Asset Management policies.

Organizational Roles, Responsibilities and Authorities

Demonstrate that the necessary level of responsibility and authority has been assigned to the asset management system. Responsibility refers to the accountability of an individual for a specific outcome, and authority refers to the legitimacy of an individual to manage or govern within a function of the asset management system.

Evidence of Compliance:

- The Asset Management Policy includes an organizational chart and "RASI" or "RACI" that clearly illustrates which individuals are responsible and have the authority for each function within the asset management system.

Level 1	Level 2	Level 3	Level 4	Level 5
No formal managerial structure for Asset Management.	Both internal and outsourced service-level roles and tasks identified and allocated.	A member of Top Management who has ultimate accountability for resources and budget is appointed to the role of Asset Manager.	Level III plus structure is aligned to the functions of the Asset Management system (i.e. Work Planning, Risk Management, Material Handling, etc.).	Level IV plus resource skills have been defined and formally documented.

Actions to Address Risks and Opportunities for the Asset Management System

Demonstrate that risk-based methodologies are used when planning the design, implementation, operation, support and improvement of the asset management system. Risk refers to stakeholder requirements and the impact that the asset management system has on organizational objectives, such as resource utilization and cost.

> Evidence of Compliance:

- The Asset Management Policy includes a risk register at various organizational levels as documented evidence of risk-based decision making methodologies that are used to assess, categorize and mitigate risk as it pertains to organizational objectives.

Level 1	Level 2	Level 3	Level 4	Level 5
No formal risk register or risk matrix exists to support Asset Management decisions.	Only a corporate-level ISO 31000 compliant risk register exists for the purpose of evaluating safety & environmental risks.	ISO 31000 compliant risk registers exist for all stakeholders, including Maintenance, that consistently define probability and consequence risks.	Level III plus risk registers are routinely used by Top Management and functional authorities to make decisions within the Asset Management system.	Level IV plus risk controls are routinely evaluated for the purpose of continuous improvement.

Asset Management Objectives

Demonstrate that each and every business function within the asset management system has specific and verifiable asset management objectives that align to the overall Strategic Asset Management Plan and organizational objectives.

Evidence of Compliance:

- Asset Management Plans are formally documented for each function within the asset management system, including design, storage, installation, operation and maintenance. These plans formally document the key activities of each function as they relate to the intended outcomes (i.e. asset capability, life cycle cost, etc.).

Level 1	Level 2	Level 3	Level 4	Level 5
Asset Management objectives are not formally documented.	Asset Management objectives exist for Maintenance and Operations only.	Partnership Agreements or similar documents exist that define the integrated role responsibilities for asset performance.	Level III plus objectives exist for Engineering and the management of maintenance, repair and operating materials.	Level IV plus a formal MOC process exists to evaluate Asset Management planning decisions against organizational objectives.

Planning to Achieve Asset Management Objectives

Demonstrate that each asset management plan is derived from a risk-based methodology and specifies the type of task needing to be performed, the individual skill or competency required to complete the task, the frequency at which the task will be performed and the method of determining if a completed task complies with the intended outcome(s).

> Evidence of Compliance:
>
> – Each Asset Management Plan is supported by a "Validation Procedure" methodology as defined by your Asset Management Policy that clearly links tasks within each plan to stakeholder requirements.

Level 1	Level 2	Level 3	Level 4	Level 5
Asset Management plans are not formally documented.	Asset Management plans exist but are based solely on OEM references as the source of key activities.	50% of in scope Assets have Validation Procedures. No monitoring process exists to verify stakeholder needs are being met.	75% of in scope Assets have Validation Procedures. Metrics are routinely reviewed to evaluate value.	Level IV plus a formal MOC process exists to evaluate Asset Management planning decisions against business objectives.

- Each Asset Management Plan includes a "Life Cycle Cost Analysis" (LCCA) as a financial justification for implementing tasks, or removing tasks in the future.

Level 1	Level 2	Level 3	Level 4	Level 5
LCCA is not routinely performed for decisions impacting the asset life cycle.	LCCA is performed on capital projects using rule of thumb guidelines.	Total Cost of Ownership is a primary driver in capital decision making. LCCA is performed using RAM modeling.	Level III plus LCCA is used to make decisions affecting Asset Management plans.	Level IV plus Top Management uses LCCA to routinely measure Asset Management plan performance.

Resources

Demonstrate that your organization has identified the internal, external and supporting resources necessary to implement Asset Management Plans. Supporting resources refers to finance, logistics, and information and data resources.

Evidence of Compliance:

- The Strategic Asset Management Plan lists the quantity and type of resource required for each key activity, including cost structure, information source and data used for decision making.

Level 1	Level 2	Level 3	Level 4	Level 5
Resource requirements are not defined within the Strategic Asset Management Plan.	RASI or RACI charts illustrate the people resource requirements for key activities defined within strategic plans.	Strategic plans identify the resources required to implement their key activities.	Resource requirements have been validated through operational acceptance testing or similar process.	Level IV plus a formal MOC process exists to evaluate resource requirements for key activities.

Demonstrate that your organization has identified the roles, responsibilities and performance expectations, including standard work, necessary to execute Asset Management Plans.

Evidence of Compliance:

- Asset Management Plans include job descriptions or other similar documents that clearly define the individual roles required to implement, maintain and continually improve the execution of plans.

Level 1	Level 2	Level 3	Level 4	Level 5
Resource requirements are not defined within the Strategic Asset Management Plan.	Roles and responsibilities have been defined and assigned to an individual.	Approved standard work instructions exist by role or function for the execution of Asset Management plans.	Level III plus standard work is routinely audited by role or function.	Level IV plus a formal MOC process exists to evaluate resource requirements for key activities.

Competence

Demonstrate a systematic approach to competency development and management. Competency refers to the knowledge, skills and behaviors of an individual that demonstrates an ability to meet the requirements of Asset Management Plans.

Evidence of Compliance:

- Each Asset Management Plan includes a "Competency Map" by role that includes the prescribed training courses, practical skill application requirements, knowledge and skill evaluation criteria, and review process for individual performance improvement.

Level 1	Level 2	Level 3	Level 4	Level 5
No standardized execution process exists and no competency requirements established for skills training.	Competencies developed by role, training records are tracked manually, and training standards are subjective and not formalized.	Competencies developed by role and activity, training records are tracked via LMS, and training standards exist for all core skills.	Level III plus training design is skills-application focused and training effectiveness is measured by performance improvement.	Level IV plus a formal MOC process exists to evaluate competency requirements relative to Asset Management plans.

Awareness

Demonstrate that people are aware of the value their role contributes to the achievement of asset management objectives and their work in relation to others within the Strategic Asset Management Plan.

Evidence of Compliance:

- Administer stakeholder surveys that evaluate the level of understanding of both asset management objectives and the relationship of roles within functional processes.

Level 1	Level 2	Level 3	Level 4	Level 5
All message channels are one-way; people are told and should understand.	Knowledge is verified for Top Management.	Knowledge is verified for most stakeholders prior to execution but not after.	Knowledge is routinely verified for <u>all</u> stakeholders during critical communiqués.	Knowledge is routinely tested to verify sustaining levels of awareness.

Communication

Demonstrate that your organization has informed both internal and external stakeholders of the value of key activities with respect to the achievement of asset management objectives.

Evidence of Compliance:

- Document the execution of "Communication Plans" defined by the Strategic Asset Management Plan.

Level 1	Level 2	Level 3	Level 4	Level 5
Email is the only delivery media and the same style is used for everyone.	Email is the only media but different styles are used for different groups.	Email and personal memos are used within varying styles for different groups. Acknowledgement of communique is documented.	Email, memos and face-to-face meetings (1/3 or total) are used with varying styles for different groups. Meeting attendance is formally documented.	Styles are matched to the individual and media formats vary with each message. Face-to-face is 50% of total effort. Surveys are used to document understanding.

There are no performance evaluation guidelines for the following requirements. The intent of these requirements is to test your organization's ability to administer asset management plans.

- "Do you have the right information and documentation to manage the assets?
- "Are you capable of adjusting asset management plans when performance is less than desired?"
- "Do controls exist to prevent unwanted changes to asset management plans and, subsequently, asset performance?"

When assessing management system performance, evidence of compliance either exists – Compliant – or does not exist – Non-compliant.

Information Requirements

Demonstrate that your organization understands which asset data and financial data is required to make informed decisions impacting asset management objectives and plans.

Evidence of Compliance:

- Document or photograph the "Daily Management Board" associated with the in-scope assets defined by the Strategic Asset Management Plan. Information requirements can be documented in the form of a metrics dashboard, scorecard, benefits tracking card, or other similar source of creating information transparency on a daily basis.

Demonstrate a formal process for the collection, validation, storage, security and retrieval of asset and financial data.

Evidence of Compliance:

- Document the Information Technology configuration management process, including Standard Operating Procedures used to enter data and report data.

Documented Information: General Requirements

Demonstrate that your organization has documented the financial, technical and regulatory information required to support your Strategic Asset Management Plan.

Evidence of Compliance:

- Document the " Validation Procedure" for each asset grouping within the scope of your Strategic Asset Management Plan.

Documented Information: Creating and Updating

Demonstrate a systematic approach to documented information and knowledge management.

Evidence of Compliance:

- Document workflow processes used to upload, approve, edit, retrieve, and audit documented information within an information management system.

Documented Information: Control

Demonstrate a systematic approach to controlling the integrity, relevance and security of documented information.

> Evidence of Compliance:

- Document the Information Technology configuration management process, including user profiles, access rights, and versioning control.

Operational Planning and Control

Demonstrate how established asset management processes, such as the identification of risk, have resulted in the modification of asset management plans in order to achieve asset management and strategic objectives.

> Evidence of Compliance:

- Document case studies in which a non-conformance occurred and asset management processes, such as root cause analysis, were used to identify a corrective action to an existing asset management plan.

Management of Change: Asset Related Changes

Demonstrate that your organization has a systematic approach to identify the risk of change associated with changes to people, resources, and the functional or physical configuration of assets.

Evidence of Compliance:

- Document the "Management of Change" process, including guidelines for assessing the size or magnitude of change (i.e. Life Cycle Cost Analysis), and provide examples of past changes and risks managed by this process.

Management of Change: Asset Management Plan Changes

Demonstrate that a formal process is routinely used to evaluate the effectiveness of asset management plans, relative to risk, and modify plans as necessary to mitigate the risk.

Evidence of Compliance:

- Document the Plan, Do, Check, Act ("PDCA") process, or similar process, and examples of changes to asset management plans managed by this process that originated outside the immediate asset owner's role.

Outsourcing

Demonstrate your organization's ability to manage risks associated with commodities or services being outsourced, including the vendor itself.

Evidence of Compliance:

- Document the "Strategic Sourcing Plan", including vendor evaluation or service level agreement criteria, that is used to evaluate commodity or service risks for each asset lifecycle within the scope of the Strategic Asset Management Plan.

- Document the Life Cycle Cost Analysis used to evaluate vendor performance, commodity or strategic sourcing alternatives.

Monitoring, Measurement, Analysis and Evaluation

Demonstrate that all stakeholders are actively involved in asset management processes and the evaluation of the achievement of asset management objectives.

Evidence of Compliance:

- Document Top Management processes for reporting financial and technical data to internal and external stakeholders, and the methods used to evaluate asset management system performance for the purpose of decision making, including meetings.

Management Review

Demonstrate how Top Management routinely audits the relevance and effectiveness of the asset management system and provides direction for continuous improvement.

Evidence of Compliance:

- Document examples of a SWOT Analysis or similar methodology used by Top Management to evaluate the relevance of stakeholders, stakeholder expectations, and the alignment of asset management objectives and plans to strategic organizational objectives.

Level 1	Level 2	Level 3	Level 4	Level 5
No analysis methodology is used to evaluate the relevance of the asset management system.	SWOT Analysis is used to identify internal constraints irrespective of market trends or external influences.	Business Planning Methodologies (Business Canvas or PEST Analysis) occasionally pulses market and business trends and reviews strategic alignment to organizational objectives.	Methodology is routinely used to evaluate the impact of business trends on organizational <u>and</u> Asset Management objectives.	Top Management understands and keeps up-to-date on business trends that affect the organizational objectives. Methodology is used to evaluate the need to change Asset Management plans.

Nonconformity and Corrective Action

Demonstrate processes are in place to identify, respond to, control and mitigate non-conformance. Non-conformance refers to unexpected asset-related incidents/accidents or failures, deviation from established processes, and undesired results for the asset management system relative to the organizational objectives.

Evidence of Compliance:

– Document the "Triggers" used to identify non-conformance and examples of investigative efforts that identified and effectively resolved the associated risks. Documentation should include evidence of a root cause analysis or similar problem solving process.

Level 1	Level 2	Level 3	Level 4	Level 5
Non-conformance is not tracked.	Failure data is tracked and analyzed on < 25% of assets impacting organizational strategic objectives.	Asset-related and non-asset related non-conformance is tracked. Stakeholder triggers are established for root cause analysis.	Level III plus advanced analysis techniques are used to resolve systemic and latent root causes.	Level IV plus Top Management monitors corrective action compliance and measures effectiveness of solutions.

Preventive Action

Demonstrate the organization's ability to proactively identify potential non-conformance (i.e. failures) in asset performance and mitigate the risk.

Evidence of Compliance:

- Document the results of RAM Analysis, Failure Mode Effects Analysis, or similar risk-based methodologies that identify failure modes and the selected risk mitigation tasks to prevent asset-related non-conformance (i.e. failures).

Level 1	Level 2	Level 3	Level 4	Level 5
No condition monitoring data exists.	Data exists but no routine reporting of known defects.	Defect severity is reported for critical assets only.	Level III plus defect severity is reported by risk mitigation task type (i.e. PdM technology) to evaluate effectiveness.	Level IV plus a formal MOC process exists to modify Asset Management plans when defect severity levels are no longer sustainable.

Continual Improvement

Demonstrate continuous improvement of the asset management system.

Evidence of Compliance:

- Document the "Organizational Change Management Plan" that is in place to quickly and easily identify opportunities for improvement and reinforce new processes and practices.

Level 1	Level 2	Level 3	Level 4	Level 5
Performance management practices are not modified to incorporate the new processes.	New processes are treated like an "add on" to the existing performance management systems.	Organizational change risks have been identified and daily management systems exist to integrate new processes and practices with legacy systems.	Level III plus Individual change risks are identified and coaching plans are in place to manage resistance.	Level IV plus Performance metrics are based on results and not activity levels.

References

ISO/TC 251 (2014). *ISO55001:2014 Asset Management -- Management Systems -- Requirements.* International Standards Organization (ISO).

Darrin J. Wikoff (2012). *Centered On Excellence: Developing Today's Business Model for Tomorrow.* MRO-Zone.

ISO/TC 262 (2009). *ISO 31000:2009 Risk management -- Principles and Guidelines.* International Standards Organization (ISO).

John S. Mitchell (2012). *Physical Asset Management Handbook.* Reliabilityweb.com.

R. Keith Mobley, Lindley R. Higgins, Darrin J. Wikoff (2008). *Maintenance Engineering Handbook, 7th Edition.* McGraw-Hill Handbooks.

U.S. Department of Health and Human Services: Food and Drug Administration (2011). *Process Validation: General Principles and Practices.*

CPSIA information can be obtained
at www.ICGtesting.com
Printed in the USA
LVHW082342170221
679458LV00003B/197